A Collection Of Christian Poems, Speeches & Skits Written For Easter And Christmas Programs

By

Pearl Robinson

Holy Fire Publishing
Oak Ridge, TN

Published by:
Holy Fire Publishing
P.O. Box 5192, Oak Ridge, TN 37831-5192
www.christianpublish.com

ISBN: 0-9763756-7-2

Printed in the United States of America and the United Kingdom

TABLE OF CONTENT

FOR EASTER

He Loves Me

Jesus loves me.
Today I am happy
And I am free.

Christ Died

I am happy
As I can be.
Christ died
For you and me.

My Savior

He is my Savior
Because he cares.
Is he yours?
If not, I will share.

You Saved My Life

When Christ died,
I told him good-bye.
He came back to life.
I told him hi.
I love you, Christ.
You saved my life.

I am Free

I am not sad.
I am not mad.
Today I am glad.
Christ died for me.
Now I am free

Christ Was Brave

You didn't give up.
You were tough.
You were brave.
Now I am saved.

He Lives

Jesus is alive.
You ask me how
I know he is alive.
He lives in my heart.

Thanks

I give you thanks.
You have done so much
For me, a little boy.
Christ, thanks a bunch.

From Me, Christ

Lots of love
To give to you,
Not from above,
From me, Christ.

I Understand

Christ, I understand
Why you died for me.
Now I am the happiest girl
In the whole world.

Loving You

Christ, loving you
Is all I want to do.
Loving you, Christ,
Is how I want to
Live my life.

Where Is Jesus?

Jesus lives in my heart.
He is also in heaven.
He watches over me.
He loves me, can't you see?

A Second Chance

I sat and watched at a glance
As Christ was nailed to the cross.
I realized I was given a second chance
To live my life free of sin
If I was willing to let Christ in.

Christ Makes Me Glad

When my friends make me sad
And my teacher says I was bad,
I can always depend on Christ.
Because he makes me glad.

He Never Complained

Jesus Christ is a strong man.
He was beaten again and again.
But he never complained.
Thanks, Christ, for enduring the pain.

My Hero

Christ is my hero.
He saved the day
And made a way
For me to go to heaven.
That makes him a hero.

He Will Return

Christ will come back.
This he has promised.
I will pray and wait
For I know he will return.

I Have To

Christ, please don't go.
What can I say or do
To save you from the cross?
"Nothing," he says. "I have to.
If I don't, your soul will be lost."

My Blessing

Christ is my blessing.
He came from heaven
Just to die for me.
He is my blessing.
Can't you see?

I Am Ready

When Christ returns
I won't have to run.
He lives in my heart,
And I am ready to leave
And go with him.
What about you?

He Left Me

I looked around for Christ,
Whom I could not see.
He left me.
Where did he go?
I know where.
He is in heaven, waiting for me.

Obey Him

If you love Christ
Because he died
To save your life,
Then obey him.
Open your heart
And let him in.

On The Cross

Christ died on the cross.
When I heard, I thought I was lost.
He arose on the third day.

He came back to life just like he said.
Accept him, for he is the only way.

Innocent Blood Shed

Christ was nailed to a cross
For this world that was lost.
He was in agony and pain as he bled.
All his innocent blood he shed.
To his heavenly Father he cried.
Then he hung his head and died.

Easter Time

I am reminded of that day
When Christ died on the cross in such a cruel way.
But I believe in my heart that Christ is alive and in heaven,
And he is seated next to God the Father
And watching over me every day.

Christ Is in Heaven

Christ lives in heaven
With God the Father.
He watches over me each day,
And I will always thank him when I pray.
Happy Easter day!

Easter Thanks

Thank you, Jesus, for what you have done.
Thank you, Jesus, for carrying your cross alone.
Thank you, Jesus, for being nailed to the cross.
Thank you, Jesus. Because of you I am not lost.

Let My Light Shine

Before I met Jesus Christ,
Darkness filled my life.
Now that I know and love him,
I am not the same.

Beaten

Christ, you were beaten,
But in your face I saw meekness.
And I never saw any tears.
Christ, you were beaten and had no fear.
You knew your heavenly Father was near.

Why for Me?

Christ, I know I shouldn't ask why.
To do what you have done tells it all.
You didn't have to do it. Why did you for me?
You saved me, and in my heart you will always be.
Your love for me is clear, I can plainly see.

Christ, Can Carry Me?

Christ carried me when I was burdened down.
He picked me up and turned me around.
He took me in his arms when I was lost.
It was then I knew why he went to the cross.
Christ carried me when I had no place to go.
Lift your head; he can do the same for you.

Christ, Please Don't Die

I stood near the cross in shock.
Standing there in disbelief,
I saw my Savior, bruised and weak.
I said to him, "Christ, please don't die."
As I began to wipe the tears from my eyes,
It was at that moment he closed his eyes and died.

My Friend

Where is Jesus Christ, my friend,

13

The one who stood by me until the end?
I want to give praises and thanks to him,
The one who died for my sins.
Thank you, my precious friend.
I love you and I will see again.

Things I Will Do for Christ

I will always love him.
I will always pray to him.
I will tell my friends about him every day.
Because of what he has done for me, I can't repay.
Christ, I love you for dying on the cross that day.

Today I Feel Blessed

A long, long time ago,
Christ died on the cross for me.
He came back to life so that I could be free.
Now he is in heaven preparing a place for me.
That is why I feel blessed today, you see.

I Honor You

Christ, you were humble.
Many times I saw you tumble
On your way to the cross.
But you always got up and
Continued up the hill.
Christ, you deserve honor,
And today I honor you.

An Empty Tomb

After the death of my Savior and Lord,
He was placed in a tomb that was borrowed.
I watched as they laid him down.

Only my heavenly Father could have known
That in three days an empty tomb would be found.
I walked to the tomb that day.
He was not there, so I ran away.
I knew in my heart he was near.
At that moment I knew I had nothing to fear.
Because Christ died, and yet he lives,
And to all who believe in him eternal life he gives.

Up Calvary Hill

Oh, how hard it must have been
To carry a cross up Calvary back then.
Christ carried his cross and never complained.
He knew he had to follow God's command.

Christ knew he would be nailed to the cross
To die and arise to save the lost.
Oh, how blessed are we when we accept him.
If we do, we are no longer bound in sin.

He Carried His Own Cross

Christ was beaten, kicked, and tossed,
And made to carry his own cross.
Through all of his suffering and pain,
He still proved to be a forgiving man.
Because he asked his Father to forgive all,
For they knew not the reason
Why he was being crucified.
Some laughed and some cried,
As Christ hung his head and died.

Today Christ Lives

One day our Savior was nailed to a cross.
He did it to save us because we were lost.
Our Savior was laughed at, mocked, and probed.
The soldiers had no shame; they gambled for his robe.

I can imagine our Savior was tired and thirsty.
They were cruel to him and offered him vinegar.
But Christ took all they did to him.
He never said one word to them.
On the ninth hour Christ was dead.
I believe that he will be back like he said.
Christ has resurrected, and today he lives.

Bound in Chains

I was born into a world full of sin.
I was bound in chains and refused to let Christ in.
I was holding on to things of the world, it seemed.
I felt dirty, unloved, and unclean.
Today my heart is filled with love.
Because I realized why he died on the cross,
And I know his blood has made me pure.
Heaven is my eternal home, I am sure.

Christ, Wait, I'll Go with You

My precious Lord and Savior,
Who came to show me favor,
I saw how you were treated.
You were kicked and beaten.
I can't bear to see you go
To Calvary's cross alone.
Christ, please wait, I'll go with you.
"No," he said. "Stay and remain true.
I will come back for my faithful few."

Christ, Can You Walk with Me?

My burdens are heavy and unbearable sometimes.
People laugh and tell me I am out of my mind
Because I believe that Christ died on the cross for me.
They say I am silly for believing that, and how could that be?
Sometimes I feel like I am all alone.

Why can't people believe what Christ has done?
Christ, my heart is heavy; can you walk with me?
"Sure," he says, "because I am the one who died to set you free."

Jesus Christ

J is for the joy that only Christ can give.
E is for the eternal life he promises us.
S is for the suffering he endured for you and me.
U is for understanding; he knows what we go through.
S is for sinlessness; he was born without sin.

C is for crucifixion; he died in such a cruel way.
H is for the hope that he gives us each day.
R is for the raised one; he rose from the dead.
I is for intercessor; he talks to God for all who believe.
S is for sacrifice; he gave his life for the world.
T is for the throne where he sits and watches all.

Christ Died for Me

One day I thought that I was lost.
I had no peace, hope, or joy.
Then I was told about an old rugged cross,
Where Christ Jesus died for me.

Now I can stand tall and be glad,
For I have happiness, love, and I'm not sad.
Thank you, God the Father, for giving your only son.
Now that I believe in Christ Jesus, my life has just begun.

Christ Lives in My Heart

Today I really feel special because Christ died for me.
He died a violent death in a sad, cruel way, you see.
But I know he still lives and is coming back one day   .
Until then I will be obedient and I will continue to pray.

Yes, today I really feel special because Christ lives in my heart.
He sent me the Holy Spirit, and no, he'll never depart.
Yes, I feel special because Jesus died on the cross.
I want you to know today that if you accept him in your life, you'll never be
lost.

Nailed to the Cross

Jesus was nailed to the cross.
He was kicked, pushed, and tossed.
There were no faults found in him.
But they still nailed him to the cross.

He was mocked, teased, laughed at, and frowned upon,
And on his head they made him wear a crown of thorns.
But to Christ that was okay
Because he knew he would rise on the third day.

Yes, they nailed him to the cross.
And today I stand before you with joy because I am not lost,
Because Christ died on the cross for me.

Easter Joy

What a joy it is to be alive on this Easter day,
To celebrate the death and resurrection of Christ
In such an honorable way.
What a joy it is to stand before all of you,
To give praise to Christ, who died for me too.

What a joy it is to hear all the poems and songs
And to feel the love everyone has in his heart.
For I know one day, when my life is over and I'll have to depart,
The joy will be knowing that I'll be with Christ my Savior.
Easter joys to everyone!

Easter Day

E is for everlasting life through Christ Jesus.
A is for all the things he has given us.
S is for Savior, because he is truly my Savior.
T is for the times I think about him over and over.
E is for excellence, for he is in every way.
R is for resurrection, for he rose on the third day.
D is for divine, because he was holy and divine when his life first began.
A is for answered prayers from Christ, my precious Savior.
Y is for yielding and letting you guide me daily, Christ Jesus.
Thank you for this wonderful day.
Happy Easter day to all!

Welcome

Welcome, welcome, welcome, this beautiful Easter day.
Welcome to the house of God, where we come to sing, worship, and pray.
Please get ready to enjoy yourselves with what we have to say.
We just want to share with you
Why Christ died on the cross that day.
Welcome, welcome, welcome, and happy Easter day!

Easter Songs

Today I am reminded of many songs.
A special one that comes to my mind is "The Old Rugged Cross."
For that is where Christ died so that we wouldn't be lost.
It is there on that cross Christ paid the ultimate cost.

Oh, and I can't forget, they crucified my Lord.
Even though he was found innocent by a man name Pilate,
He was given back to the people, and someone yelled, "Crucify him!"
Then the crowd took him and beat him all night long.
The next day they lead him up a hill to Calvary, carrying his cross alone.

But he arose! He arose!
Yes, he rose from the dead for me.
He ascended into heaven, feeling no pain.
And he left his Holy Spirit to comfort me until he comes again.

He Gave His Life

Christ gave his life for you and me.
Now I know his love for me is real.
He knew his life he had to give.
For them who believe in him would die, yet live.
Who else would be willing to give their life for me, a sinner?
God had his only son die because his kingdom he wants me to enter.
He loves me so much, he made a way for me to live forever.
But that can only happen through Christ, who died to make life better.

If Christ Hadn't Died

I was born into a world full of sin.
I had no desire in my heart to let Christ in.
In my mind I didn't need anything.
And oh, what happy songs I would sing.

But now I know if Christ hadn't died,
I would be lost, with nowhere to hide.
And because he died, today I am free
To love him because he did it for me.

If Christ hadn't died on Calvary's cross,
We would all be confused, bound and lost.
But because of our heavenly Father's mercy,
We all have eternal life if we believe
That Christ was once dead, but now he lives.

Forgive Me, Christ

Christ, I've done many bad things in my life—
Things that I'm ashamed of and things that weren't so nice.
Christ, how can I come to you when you are so perfect?
I'm ashamed of the things I've done; some I can't correct.
But someone told me about your dying on the cross for me.
I said, "I didn't deserve it. Why would he?"

Christ, it took a long time for me to understand and see
Why you willingly went to the cross and died that day.
But I know now that you did it to take my sins away.
Christ, I accept you today with all my heart.
Please forgive me for all the wrong I've done.
I realize now, Christ, that you are the only one.

Where Would I Be?

If Christ hadn't died on the cross,
I would be in this sinful world lost.
There would be no happiness and no joy.
I would really be an unhappy boy.

But since he did die that day,
I will always be thankful in a special way.
I want to be more like him every day.
And I won't forget to thank him every time I pray.

They Crucified My Son

My name is Mary; I'm the mother of Jesus.
I was there on that sad, sad, day.
I watched as my son was treated in such a cruel way.
They beat, kicked, and mocked him, and all I could do was pray.

They crucified my son on the cross
So the world wouldn't be lost.
On that day he wore a purple robe,
And they placed on his head a crown made of thorns.

He was placed on a cross between two thieves.
I watched in disbelief and fell to my knees,
Because in my son they found no fault.
He was able to conquer death, hell,
And the grave so our souls wouldn't be lost.

Christ Resurrected

I know that Christ rose from the dead,
Because he lives in my heart and I talk to him before I go to bed.
He leads me and guides me day and night.
He makes sure that I always do what is right.

I know Christ rose on the third day,
Because his tomb was found empty, they say.
No one knew what had happen or where he had gone,
Because he was last seen in the tomb alone.

Christ had resurrected and was among his disciples.
At first they didn't believe that it was Jesus.
Then he showed them his hands; it was then they knew the man
Had resurrected and come to be with them again.

I Will Honor and Praise You, Christ

Christ, I honor you because God gave you, his only son,
And because of that you hung, bled, and died.
Christ, I honor you because through accepting your death and resurrection,
My life has just begun.
I honor you because you are the way, the truth, and the life.

Christ, I praise you because you saved my soul.
I praise you because through you the truth was told.
Christ, I praise you for teaching me to do what is right.
All praises and honors to you, Christ, because through you I can now see
the light.

He Is Coming Back

Some believe Christ never died
On the cross,
So therefore, how could he
Come back to life?

Some say he is not a Savior,
That he is just a man

22

To whom God showed favor.

But I stand before you today
To tell you Christ did die on the cross,
And he resurrected on the third day.

If you don't believe that he did,
Your soul is already lost.
Christ is coming back
For me and all who believe, and that is a fact.

My Prayer to Christ

Christ, I thank you for what you did
When you were nailed to the cross.
You did exactly what you said.
You took my sins along with you.
Christ, I thank you because you didn't have to die.
You obeyed your heavenly Father and did it anyway.
I thank you, Christ, for being my Lord and Savior.
Christ, I thank you for showing me unmerited favor.
Christ, I thank you, this I pray.

A Letter to Christ

Dear Christ,

I want to thank you today for what you have done for me. I know you didn't have to do it, but you loved me so much that you suffered and died for me. Christ, I really feel sad for what they did to you and how you were treated. I know you gave your life for me, and that is why I accept you in my heart and I will love you always. Christ, sometimes I think about how you died for me and I feel like my love is not enough. I want to abide in you and I want you to abide in me. I want to be more like you each day because you have given me a gift that is more precious than gold. Thanks to you, I have the gift of salvation. Christ, thanks for dying on the cross for me that day a long, long time ago. One day I will see you in heaven.

Love,
Pearl

Thanks to God the Father

Heavenly Father, I stand before you today
To give all praises and thanks to you in a humble way.
For I know in my heart that you didn't have to give your only son
To die that day when he did nothing wrong.

Heavenly Father, I thank you for loving me so dearly.
I know, when you sat and watched from your great throne,
That you were pleased with what your son had done.
He made you very glad, for he listened and he obeyed.

Heavenly Father, my love for you will never die.
In Christ, your son, I will always abide.
For I know he died so sad and cruel as he hung very high.
And now he has resurrected and is seated on the throne next to you.
Thank you, God the Father.

An Easter Prayer

My heavenly Father, we want to give all honor and praise to you. Father, we thank you for this Easter day, for it is the time of year when we can sit and think about our Lord and Savior and what he has done for us. Father, we want to thank you for allowing your only begotten son to go to the cross and die for sinners like us. Father, we didn't deserve it and we thank you. He not only went to the cross and died , but you raised him from the dead so that we may have eternal life if we believe in him. Father, we thank you for being such a loving God, for we know that you didn't have to do it, but you did because you love us more than anything. We want to do what is pleasing to you.

Now, Father, we ask that you would bless this program and all of the participants. And Father, we pray that if there is anyone here who does not know you, that person would come to know you through this program. Father, we thank you and we ask it all in Christ's name. Amen.

FOR CHRISTMAS

Born to Die

Jesus was born
To die for me,
And now I am free.

Born to Die

Jesus was born
To die for me,
And now I am free.

Hail to the King

He will bring joy
To every girl and boy.
Hail to the King.
A happy song I'll sing.

Christ Makes Me Smile

I am a happy child.
Christ talks to me.
When I am sad,
Christ makes me smile.

Thanks to God

Christ was born
To be with me.
Thanks to you, God,
I am never alone.

A Baby for Me

I am only three.
I really want to see
This baby God sent,
A baby just for me.

Where Is this Baby?

I heard about a baby
Born of a virgin lady,
He who was born free of sin.
Where is this baby?

God's Only Son

A baby was born,
God's only son.
A baby was born
To bear the cross
All alone.

I Will

I will give you thanks.
I will give you praise.
I will give you honor
Just because you were born.

He Brought Joy

A little baby boy,
One who brought joy
Into my little heart.
Thank you, God, you are smart.

Baby Jesus

Baby Jesus was born free of sin.
Open your heart and let him in.
Baby Jesus was born to be loved.
He is a gift from heaven above.

Lots of Love

A sweet baby boy,
He had so much joy
And lots of love
To share with all
From God above.

Holy and Divine

A precious baby born to be mine,
One who was born holy and divine.
Christ was perfect in every way.
I live to be more like him each day.

Christ's Birth Makes Me Happy

When I heard of his birth,
I was the happiest girl on earth.
Thank you, little baby Jesus.
Your birth made me happy.

My Blessing

Christ is my blessing.
He came from heaven
Just to die for me.
He is my blessing.
Can't you see?

I Am Ready

When Christ returns
I won't have to run.
He lives in my heart,
And I am ready to leave
And go with him.
What about you?

He Left Me

I looked around
For Christ, whom
I could not see.
He left me; where did he go?
He is in heaven,
Waiting for me.

Christmas, a Time to Share

Christmastime is here.
Christmas is a time to share,
A time to show all you care.
God cared; he gave us his only son.
God shared his love with everyone.

Welcome

Welcome, welcome, welcome.
Sit back, enjoy, and be blessed
As we tell you the real reason
For this happy holiday season.

Who Is this Baby Jesus?

He is God's only begotten son,
Born to bear our sins alone.
He is our precious Lord and Savior,
The one who came to show us favor.

I Love You, Christ

You were born for me,
And you came to set me free.
I love you, Christ,
Because you have changed my life.
Thank you for being born,
God's only begotten son.

One Who Was Blessed

Christ was blessed
By God his Father
From the time he was born,
For he was God's only son.
Christ never had to fear.
Because God was always near.

I Was a Baby

I am four years old.
I was a baby, I've been told.
I am a little too small
For those memories.
I really can't recall.
But I do remember a baby
Born to be my only Savior.

A Silent Night

As the day turned into darkness
And the stars shone bright,
There was stillness about.
It was a holy and silent night.
That is when our Savior was born.
He was born for all to see the light.

A Time for Giving

Christmas is a time for giving
And also a time for believing
In the one and only divine being,
The one whom God gave to save us all.
Please accept this gift when he calls.
He is the only answer for the world today.
Give him your heart and he'll never go away.

A Holy Night

It was a holy night.
The stars shined bright.
Everything seemed so right.
A precious baby was born.
Oh, what a beautiful sight.
As he slept in his manger quietly,
Mary and Joseph looked on proudly.
For they knew with all their hearts,
A King was born on this holy night.

Born to Save All

A baby born holy and divine,
One whom I can surely call mine,
He came to give me peace.
He came to give me joy.
This precious little baby boy
Was born to save all.
Please come to him when you hear his call.

Merry Christmas

Merry Christmas to one and all.
To us a baby was born, so tiny and small.
He will bring us peace and joy.
God has blessed the world
With his holy gift: a baby boy.
Merry Christmas, and God bless all.

A King Was Born

One night many years ago,
A baby was born with a special glow.
Only our heavenly Father could have known
That on that night a King would be born.

This King was born without sin.
Please open your heart and let him in.
Why live your life in the night
When a King was born to give you light?

The Greatest Gift

I was given a special gift from Mom.
Dad gave me all the things I asked for.
My grandma and grandpa gave me lots of love.
But the greatest gift came from heaven above.
That gift was my precious Lord and Savior.
Accept him today and God will grant you favor.

Born without Sin

Christ was born without sin.
He is the only one who can take sins away.
But we have to open our hearts and let him in.
Christ loves us and He proved it one day
By going to the cross in a humble way.
He didn't have to do it, but he did because he loves us.
If he hadn't died, our lives would be a mess.
Christ, we love you and you are the best.

Christ, You Can Have My Bed

I heard about a baby who was born with no bed.
He had nowhere to sleep and no place to lay his little head.
I was always taught to share.
Christ, because of your birth, I care.
It's okay; you can have my bed.
God will bless me with another one, he said.

Hated by Many; Loved by Few

Jesus, who was born King of the Jews,
Had a passion for telling the good news.
He knew he was hated by many and loved by few.
People talked about and mocked him, this he knew.
But Christ showed his love for everyone
By going to the cross, God's only son.

Hated by the King

When the king heard of his birth,
He wanted to search all parts of the earth.
He wanted baby Jesus found and bought to him.
But God knew the king's heart.
He knew the king hated Christ.
So God sent angels to have Joseph depart.
They left the town of David for a new start.

A Holy Baby

I came to worship a holy baby,
One who was born in a stable,
Worthy of worship and praises,
A holy baby born our Lord and Savior.
Thank you, God, because you saw a need
To send your son into a world so full of sin,
To save us and to be our best friend.

Let Us Worship this Baby

Some will hate this baby.
Some will love this baby.
Some will want to kill this baby.
This baby will bless some.
But I say to everyone,
Let us all worship this baby.

The Greatest Gift

I have received many gifts.
Some of them I have kept.
Some made me laugh,
And some made me weep.
But the greatest gift of all
Was the one God gave out of love.
Jesus is that gift sent from heaven above.

An Amazing Birth

God showed favor to a woman one day.
He knew his son's birth was the only way
To save his people from sins they were born in.
Christ was conceived miraculously.
That is what made his birth so amazing.
A holy baby born of a virgin.

The Lord Has Come

A Savior was promised to all,
One whom we should answer when he calls.
He was born to pay a debt that we owe,
No matter whether you are rich or poor,
A debt that when he dies we will owe no more.
The Lord was born to pay the price.
The debt will be paid with his life.
He has come so you can live.
Born to die, his life he was willing to give.

Bound by Sin

Before Christ, our Savior, was born,
I was bound by sin and my heart was torn.
I didn't know which way to go,
And I didn't know who to ask or what to do.
But now that Christ, my Savior, is here,
I can go anywhere without fear.
Christ, since I opened my heart and let you in,
I am no longer bound by my sins.

Welcome

Welcome to the house of the Lord.
We have poems, songs, and more.
Sit back, open your heart, and enjoy.
Before you leave you will understand
What was so special about this baby boy.
Welcome, one and all.

God, Are You Happy?

God, you gave us your son.
Now you are in heaven alone.
God, are you happy or sad?
Please tell me you are glad.
I have accepted your son,
And I don't mind sharing
Him with you,
Because you are so caring.
God, are you happy?
I am.

Thank You for Coming

You have heard poems read from our hearts.
You have heard how Christ can give you a new start.
You have seen the joy we have in knowing Christ.
You have heard the children singing.
Now we want to thank you for coming. Thank you and God bless you.

Christmastime

A time to give all thanks and praises
To Christ, who was born to be our Savior.
Mary, upon whom God showed great favor,
Was blessed when she chose to carry our Savior.

A time to reflect on God's precious gift,
And a time to give thanks to him for his kindness.
You can give me gold or silver,
But no one can out-give God, the greatest giver.

Miracle Baby

The baby everyone traveled far to see,
The one who would set us free.
Who is this miracle baby?
He is our Lord and Savior.

Born of a virgin woman,
He was loved before his life began.
Who is this miracle baby?
He is our Great Comforter.

Let Us Worship this Baby

He who was born into this world,
The one who should be praised and loved,
Let every man, woman, boy, and girl,
Worship this holy baby,
The one who was born of a virgin lady.

God knew he wanted Mary to carry
And give birth to his only son.
Let us worship and share the news.
For this baby would be crowned King of the Jews
And one day suffer and die to save the world .

Let us worship this baby boy
Because he came to bring us true joy.

Bound by Sin

Before Christ, our Savior, was born,
I was bound by sin and my heart was torn.
I didn't know which way to go,
And I didn't know who to ask or what to do.
But now that Christ, my Savior, is here,
I can go anywhere without fear.
Christ, since I opened my heart and let you in,
I am no longer bound by my sins.

My Christmas List for Christ

Christ, can you help me to save my friend,
Who has a broken heart and feels there is no end?
Christ, will you heal all who are sick
So they can rejoice on this Christmas day?
Christ, can you visit the homeless
And tell them their lives aren't such a mess?
Christ, can you stop by the homes of the poor
And let them know if they trust you, they will have more?
Christ, please, can you visit the people in jail

And tell them to trust you and you won't let them fail?
Lastly, Christ, can you turn to your left
And tell my heavenly Father I love him and he is the best?

My Christmas Wish

I wish I could be just like you, Christ—
Full of joy, peace, and life.
I wish I could save the world one day,
If only they would listen to what I have to say.
I wish I hadn't been born in sin.
But I know if I open my heart and let Christ in,
He will take my sins away.
I wish I were in heaven with my Savior,
The one who asks God to show me favor.
I wish I could meet God in person
And give him thanks for what he has done,
For he has given me a gift that is better than gold.
Christ is that gift, given freely to us and not sold.

Christmas Night

C is for Christ, who was born on a quiet night.
H is for heaven, where he would return one day.
R is for rest; Christ lay asleep on the hay.
I is for innocent baby, born to set the world free.
S is for Savior, one who would die to save you and me.
T is for the tears of joy that flowed from his mother's face.
M is for the manger where he rested quiet that night.
A is for the angels who watched over Christ, our Savior.
S is for the stars that shone so beautiful and bright.

N is for the newborn babe who would die for us.
I is for intercessor, for he wants God to show us favor.
G is for given, unto us a precious Savior.
H is for the holy one, a gift from heaven above.
T is for thanks to God for his gift of love.

No Place to Call Home

Our Lord and Savior was born in a stable,
Given birth by a woman who was favored.
He had no place to lay his head.
His mother found a manger and made it his bed.
There he lay peacefully upon the hay.
Mary closely watched as he lay.
He had no place to call his home.
But God, his Father, never left him alone.
For he was proud of his only son
Who would one day sit next to him
In his heavenly home,
Seated next to the Father on the throne.

A Baby, a Savior

What an honor it must have been
To be born a holy baby for all to see,
A special baby for the world to love,
A beautiful baby sent from heaven above,
A baby born to be worshiped by all,
A Savior who was born to save the world,
A Savior who knew he would die on the cross,
A Savior who conquered death, hell, and the grave,
A Savior who returned with the keys in his hands,
A Savior who knew his Father's divine plan,
Which is to give eternal life to every man.

Christmas Memories

A baby born on a cold Christmas night,
A baby born in a stable, lying in a manger,
A baby who brought joy to the shepherds,
A baby born to be King of Kings and Lord of Lords,
A baby born to be King of the Jews,
A baby who brought the world good news,
A baby who was born son of the Most High,
A baby who would be called a Wonderful Counselor,

A baby who would bring peace to us on earth,
A baby who was born of a virgin birth,
A baby born of a woman to whom God showed favor,
That baby is Christ, our Lord and Savior.

A Gift from Heaven

I have received gifts from my father and mother.
I was also given gifts by my sister and brother.
But what a blessing to receive a gift from heaven,
A gift I will always treasure.
My heavenly Father took such pleasure.
He gave us a gift so undeserving
For all to unwrap and receive,
A gift that will bring salvation if you believe.
If you accept this gift, it can't be returned.
But if you don't, in the fire you will burn.
This gift from heaven will bring you peace.
Please accept it, for it is yours to keep.

Jesus Loves Me

He was born to set me free
From all the sins I carried within.
Jesus loves me, I can plainly see.
He died on the cross
Just to show how much he loves the lost.
A little baby born to be a comforter;
God must really care for me.
He made a way for me to enter
Into his glorious and beautiful kingdom.
Yes, Jesus loves me,
And I know the day will come
When he will say to me, "Well done."

Born in a Stable

The Savior of this world
Was born in a stable.
There in a manger he lay,
So wonderfully made.

The night was silent and cold.
He was wrapped in swaddling clothes
As he lay gently upon a pile of hay,
Born to save the world one day.

Yes, he was born in a stable.
There he lies, so gentle and small.
God, his Father, was with him through it all,
And today Christ is with us until forever.

The Shepherds Saw an Angel Too

While Mary was giving birth
To the one who would be called the Christ,
She knew that from heaven above,
God was looking down with great love.

As the shepherds watched their flocks by night,
An angel came to them and said, "Don't be afraid.
For in the city of David is born a new babe,
One who will command us to do what is right."

The shepherds felt such peace and joy,
They wanted to see this special boy
Who would one day be crowned
King of Kings and Lord of Lords.

Born to Die for You and Me

An innocent newborn baby,
So precious to his mother, Mary,
Was born to die for you and me
And to set the world free.

42

This one was worshiped by all.
King of all Kings, he was called.
Everyone rejoiced when they heard the news.
This newborn baby would be King of the Jews.

Oh, what peace you should have,
Knowing the reason for his birth.
For he was born here on earth
To suffer and die for us.

.

Underneath the Stars

There lay a little baby boy,
One who would be called Wonderful.
He would bring the world joy.
In a tiny manger he lay,
Beautiful and wonderfully made.
Underneath the stars that night,
A Savior was born to show us light,
And he will guide us to do what is right.

Follow that Star

From the east I saw a star.
This star stood out from afar.
It was shining brighter than the others.
I gathered all I had together
And left home to followed that star.
I traveled many nights and many days,
Not letting anything get in my way.
I had to understand why
That one star stood out.
I got there and stood underneath that special star.
I saw it was shining upon a special baby boy.
At that moment my heart was filled with joy.
I was glad I followed that star,
One that seemed so very far.

Thank You, God

Thank you, God, for the divine plan you have.
Thank you for the one and only son you gave.
Thank you for his birth on that holy Christmas night.
Thank you because he came to give the world light.

Thank you for being so kind and merciful.
Thank you, God; I know it must be painful
To send your son to be born in a world so sinful.
Thank you, God, because you knew what he would go through.

And when it is all done, he will only be loved by a few.
Thank you, God, that you loved me enough to send
Your one and only son to be my divine friend.
Thank you, God, that when my life is over, I will see you in the end.

A Christmas Prayer

Father, first we want to give all honor and praise to you. We thank you for you kindness and your mercy. Father, we thank you for sending your only son to be born into a world that is hateful, mean, and full of sin. Father, we know you didn't have to allow him to be born upon this earth to be hated by so many, but you did and we thank you for that. We thank you for Jesus Christ, who was born to save us. Father, we thank you for this gift you have given us, a precious gift of love. Father, we don't deserve it, but we thank you for him.

Now, Father, I ask that you bless this program and all the participants. I pray that it will touch someone and that he or she will ask, "What must I do to be saved?" In Christ's name I pray. Amen.

SKITS

A Walk to the Crucifixion
Cast: Two kids, age ten through twelve

Person 1—I was there that morning when it all started.

Person 2—You mean when Christ was brought before the governor?

Person 1—Yes. I was among the crowd that yelled, "Crucify him!" But I remained silent. The governor found no fault in Christ, but the crowd wanted him dead and they all yelled, "Crucify him!"

Person 2—I thought there were two men and the crowd had to choose one who would live.

Person 1—Yes. They chose Christ to die and the sinner to go free.

Person 2—So they are going to kill an innocent man?

Person 1—Yes. And I want to be near him and show him that I am here if he needs me. So I will follow him up Calvary's hill.

Person 2—But Christ won't know that you are in the crowd.

Person 1—You're probably right.

Person 2—I will walk with you

Person 1—Christ is a good man. He loves everybody and he has done so much for us.

Person 2—It is such a shame they want to kill him. He has done nothing wrong, yet he is going willingly.

Person 1—Someone told me he is doing this because it is the will of his Father.

Person 2—But how can a father let his son be nailed to a cross and die in such a horrible way and not try to help him?

Person 1—For us.

Person 2—What do you mean?

Person 1—Right now, we are sinners and we are lost in our sins. God loves us and doesn't want death to be our final destiny. So he sent his only son to die for all of our sins.

Person 2—Oh, wow! What a merciful and loving God to allow his one and only son to die for a sinner like me.

Person 1—I also heard that Christ will not stay dead. He will rise in three days.

Person 2—Wait a minute, now. You are scaring me. I thought once you die you were gone forever.

Person 1—That is true, but there is something different about Christ. He has the power to do all things.

Person2—What do you mean? What things can he do?

Person 1—I have heard about some of his miracles. He raised people who were dead, healed the sick, and fed the homeless.

Person 2—So will he raise himself from the dead?

Person 1—No, but his heavenly Father will. He has all power in his hands.

Person 2—What will happen when Christ comes back to life? What will he do? Where will he go?

Person 1—He will be among his people for a few days to comfort them. Then he will ascend into heaven to be seated on the throne with his Father. But he will leave his Holy Spirit to live in all believers.

Person 2—When you say, "believers," whom exactly are you talking about?

Person 1—Believers are people who believe with all their hearts that Jesus is God's son and he was raised from the dead. They realize that they are sinners and have faith in Christ that he can and will forgive them for their sins.

Person 2—If they believe these things, they will be saved and have eternal life through Christ?

Person 1—Yes.

Person 2—Let me make sure I understand. God loves us, and because of his love and mercy, he is giving us a free gift of salvation, and all who accept the gift will have everlasting life.

Person 1—Yes. It is just that simple. As easy as saying, "One, two three."

Person 2—Can you tell me about heaven, hell, and the lake of fire?

Person 1—Those places are all real, though some people may tell you that they are not. Heaven is where all believers' souls will rest until the day of judgment. It is a beautiful place of lightness, happiness, and joy. Hell is where non-believers' souls will be tormented until Judgment Day. It's a place of darkness and sadness. Once you are there, all hope is lost. The eternal lake of fire is real. All who have rejected Christ will go there once they have been judged. They will be thrown into the lake of fire along with Satan, and they will all die a second death and will be separated from God forever.

Person 2—Wow! What an earful. Who in their right mind would want to go there when all they have to do is accept God's free gift of salvation?

Person 1—It is sad, but many people have and will continue to reject Christ because of their selfish pride and lust for the things of the world.

Person 2—Before talking to you, I didn't know what all this meant or why Christ had to die, but now I understand. I understand the plan of salvation. I have to accept Christ as my Savior if I want to see him again.

Person 1—That's right. You know, while we have been talking, the crucifixion has taken place. Christ has died.

Person 2—I am not sad anymore because I know he is coming back for me one day because I am a true believer.

Person 1—It's great Christ is not suffering anymore, and I know he will be resurrected in a few days. I'm not sad anymore either. We'll both see him again.

Both—Christ, we love you and we have accepted your death and resurrection. (to the audience) Have you?

I Must Die

Cast: Christ and a girl or boy age six through eight

Girl—Christ, I heard about you when you were born.

Christ—What did you hear, my child?

Girl—I heard you were born in a manager and you were born to die for me.

Christ—Yes, I came so you can have everlasting life.

Girl—Christ, what is everlasting life, and why will you die to give it to me?

Christ—Everlasting life is life after death, and I must die so you and all the people in the world who accept me can live forever.

Girl—But Christ, I am alive. We are all living.

Christ—My precious child, I know you are alive and I am alive too. But before you can have everlasting life, I must die.

Girl—Who told you that you must die?

Christ—My Father in heaven said that I must die for you.

Girl—You mean, you will die for me?

Christ—Yes, my little one, and for all the rest of the world.

Girl—Is God okay with you doing that?

Christ—Yes. It is his divine will for my life while I am here.

Girl—How will you die?

Christ—I will die on a cross

Girl—Can you tell me again why you are doing this?

Christ—I am doing this to take your sins and all the other people's sins to the cross with me so you won't have to live in them anymore.

Girl—My sins? What do you mean?

Christ—Well, do you always listen to your parents? Do you tell the truth all the time?

Girl—No, sir, I don't.

Christ—Those are sins that I must die for.

Girl—Christ, you are really nice.

Christ—There is something else I must tell you. When I die I won't stay dead. I will come back to life.

Girl—Wow! How can you do that?

Christ—I can't, but my Father can. He has the power to do all things.

Girl—Where is your Father?

Christ—My Father lives in heaven and he watches over us every day.

Girl—You mean, when I do bad things he can see me?

Christ—Yes, he can, for he sees all things.

Girl—Is he my Father too?

Christ—He is your heavenly Father also.

Girl—When you take my sins away after you die on the cross, will I sin again?

Christ—Yes, you will, for you are not perfect. But because I will go to the cross and die for your sins, you have the right, if you believe in me, to ask me for forgiveness. I will then talk it over with my Father and he will forgive you if you meant it from the bottom of your little heart.

Girl—What happens if I continue to sin?

Christ—God will be unhappy with you and he will have to punish you. But if you believe in me, your goal should be to try to sin no more.

Girl—I love you, Christ, and I don't want to make God mad. I will always try to do what is right.

Christ—This will be pleasing to my Father

Girl—Christ, when you come back to life, where will you go?

Christ—I will go back to heaven to be with my heavenly Father. I will sit on the throne with him, watching the good and the bad.

Girl—Can I go with you?

Christ—No, my child, not now. But one day you will, because I will prepare a place for all who believe in me.

Girl—When I need to talk to you, can I?

Christ—Yes, my precious child, you can always talk to me. When I leave here, I will leave my Holy Spirit to live in you and comfort you.

Girl—So I won't be alone?

Christ—No, my precious child. I will always be in your heart, loving you and guiding you to do what is right. May joy and peace be with you until I see you again.

Girl—Good-bye, Christ. I love you. And I will tell all the people I know and meet about you and the good news you have shared with me.

We Can Save Christ—I Know We Can

Setting: The day before the crucifixion

Cast: Four people *(age nine to twelve)* and the voice of God

Person 1—Have you all heard the news about our Lord and Savior?

Person 2—No, what news?

Person 3—I heard something about a crucifixion.

Person 4—Yeah. They are going to kill our Lord and Savior.

Person 1—That is the news. We must save him.

Person 2—Why will they kill him? What has he done?

Person 3—Christ is innocent. He didn't do anything wrong. He has never hurt anybody. He is a good man.

Person 4—I don't understand. If he is such a good man and has done nothing wrong, why should he die?

Person 1—I don't know, but he must.

Person 2—I am so confused. Christ has done nothing but good things.

Person 3—Yeah. He healed the sick, and he made the blind see and the lame walk.

Person 4—If he has done all these good things, why should he die?

Person 1—Guys, we can't let him die. We must save him. I know we can.

Person 2—How? We don't know where he is or what he is doing.

Person 3—Wherever he is, he is probably scared and sad. We have to find him and save him. I know we can.

Person 4—Where will we go to look for him?

Person 1—I know he is somewhere in the town of Jerusalem. He is not alone because there are twelve men who follow him. I hope they will protect him until we can find him.

Person 2—We have to hurry because we don't have a lot of time. We have to get to him before the Roman soldiers do.

Person 3—Before we leave, let's pray to our heavenly Father and ask him to lead us to Christ. Surely he would want to save his son.

Person 4—Yes, let's pray. Father God, please lead and guide us to our Lord and Savior. If we don't get to him, he will be crucified and we don't understand why. Can you help us find him? He is your son and I know you want to save him. Please help us. Amen.

God—My precious children, my son is innocent and I know he has done nothing wrong. But he is doing my will, and that is to die on the cross to save the world.

Person 1—But how will his death save the world?

God—Right now all people are lost in their sins, and my son is the only hope for everyone. I have sent him down from heaven to save the world. He must die on the cross. I love you so much I am willing to let my son die so you can be forgiven for your sins and have eternal life though Christ, my son.

Person 2—So Christ has to die and we can't save him?

God—Yes, he must die, for that is my will. But he will resurrect on the third day and will ascend back into heaven to be with me. He will be seated at my right hand forever, interceding for all who believe in him.

Person 3—So Christ is going to die, but he will come back to life and we can still talk to him and he will always be our Savior?

God—Yes, Christ will always be your Savior. When he leaves you, he will leave his Holy Spirit to abide in all who accept him. And he will always be the light of the world.

Person 1—Well, guys, I guess we don't have to save him after all. God has spoken to us, and now we know that Christ must die for us. It is God's will.

Person 2—I am so happy that Christ loves me that much. He is willing to die for me. I sure don't feel like I deserve it.

Person 3—We don't have to save him; God will save him by bringing him back to life. Wow! This news is so awesome, I just want to scream.

Person 4—God is the best. He is willing to give his one and only son to die for us on the cross so that if we believe in him we will have eternal life. That is great news.

Person 1—I believe!

Person 2—I believe!

Person 3—I believe!

Person 4—I believe!

All—God bless you, and happy Easter!

We Must Go Tell the Good News
Setting: The Night Christ Was Born
Cast: one girl, two boys

Girl—This night is so quiet and beautiful, it just feels different.

Boy 1—I know. Even the stars are shining brighter than normal.

Girl—There's a stillness about this night.

Boy 1—What do you think is going on?

Girl—I don't have a clue.

Boy 2—Haven't you all heard the good news about the baby?

Girl—What baby?

Boy 1—What news can be so good that it could make this night so different?

Boy 2—In the city of David, in an old stable, a Savior has been born, and he is asleep in a manger.

Girl—What do you mean, a Savior has been born?

Boy 1—Whom was he born to save? And from what?

Boy 2—He was born to save the world from the penalty of their sin.

Girl—Sin? I've never heard that word.

Boy 1—Neither have I. Can you tell us what sin is?

Boy 2—Sin is doing something that God says not to do.

Girl—Oh. You mean, like when you don't listen to your parents?

Boy 1—Or if you steal something?

Boy 2—Yes. God is not happy when we do such things.

Girl—*(smiling)*How can a baby save the world?

Boy 1—Yeah! That sounds crazy. A baby who can save the world? That's really funny!

Boy 2—Well, if you want to see for yourselves, just follow me to the stable. When you see him, then you will believe me.

Girl—*(looking through a peephole)* Hey! I see that special baby and his mother, and I just want to bow down and worship him!

Boy 1—*(looking through another peephole)* I don't believe it! There is a baby lying in a manger, and there is something special about him. I will bow down and worship him too!

Boy 2—When I saw him I bowed down and worshiped him also. I felt he was worthy of worship and praise.

Girl—The moment I saw that baby with his mother, my heart changed.

Boy 1—You know, I didn't believe you, but this baby has changed my heart too.

Boy 2—Now that we have seen this baby and worshiped him, we must go out and tell everyone the good news.

Girl—What will we say about him?

Boy 1—And how should we say it?

Boy 2—*(to the girl)* When you saw the baby, you bowed down and worshiped him.

Boy 2—*(to the boy)* And you did the same thing. You both had a feeling of joy that only Christ could have given you.

Girl and Boy 1—But what does all that mean?

Boy 2—It means that only Christ can change your heart.

Girl—Yes, but what is the good news?

Boy 2—This tiny baby brings eternal life to all who believe in him. He is a gift from God our Father, who loves us so much he is willing to give us a way to be forgiven of ours sins through Christ, this baby who will die for us one day.

Girl—That is awesome news!

Boy 1—Are you saying this baby will die for the whole world one day?

Boy 2—Yes. And on the third day he will arise and will then ascend into heaven and wait there for all believers.

Boy 1—And if we believe these things we will have eternal life?

Boy 2—Yes! That is the good news that we must go and tell.

Girl—Wow! I never had anyone die for me before. I will go and tell all the girls about this Savior.

Boy 1—I will go and tell all the boys.

Boy 2—And I will tell the rest of the people about this Savior who was born to save the people of this world if they will only believe.

All—Let us all go and tell the good news. He has come to save us. Merry Christmas to all!

A Free Gift

Cast: Two children, age six, having a conversation when Christ was born

Child 1—Hey! I was given a free gift for Christmas.

Child 2—No way! Nobody gets a free gift; our parents have to buy them.

Child 1—Not the gift I'm talking about. This one is really free.

Child 2—Can you tell me where my parents can get this gift? Sometimes when I ask for things, they say, "We don't have any money." Surely they wouldn't complain about a free gift.

Child 1—I'll be happy to tell you how to receive this free gift.

Child 2—Where can I go to get it? What store is it in?

Child 1—This gift is not in a store.

Child 2—Then how can I get it?

Child 1—The free gift that I got for Christmas is baby Jesus, who was born on Christmas day, and I believe with all my heart that he is the son of God.

Child 2—A baby? What makes him a gift?

Child 1—He was born to give the gift of salvation.

Child 2—Salvation? I have no idea what you are talking about.

Child 1—Have you heard of heaven?

Child 2—Yes. I've heard my parents talk about it a few times.

Child 1—Do you want to go to heaven when you die?

Child 2—Not if I have to die to get there.

Child 1—Well, we all have to die one day, and you make the choice where you want to spend your eternal life while you are living.

Child 2—Yes, I would choose heaven. I've heard that my grandmother is there, and I would love to see her again.

Child 1—Well, before you can get there, you have to accept this gift Christ came to give you.

Child 2—How do I accept this free gift?

Child 1—Just believe in your heart that Jesus is God's son and that he was born to die on the cross for your sins and God will raise him from the dead.

Child 2—Hey, wait a minute! You never talked about Christ being dead and coming back to life.

Child 1—Christ was born to die for our sins, and he will come back to life.

Child 2—So, if I believe, I will receive this free gift?

Child 1—Yes.

Child 2—Wow! This is so easy.

Child 1—Do you believe with all your heart?

Child 2—Yes, I do.

Child 1—Now that you have accepted the free gift that Christ came to give, you are on your way to heaven.

Child 2—Will I see my grandmother again?

Child 1—Yes, you will.

Child 2—Can I give this gift to my mom and dad?

Child 1—No, but Christ can. All you have to do is tell them why Christ was born and that he will one day die for them. It's up to them to accept Christ as their free gift from God.

Child 2—I will tell them because I really want to see them in heaven.

Child 1—That is the best news you can share with anybody. Go out and tell your friends! They may not know about baby Jesus. May God bless you, and have a merry Christmas!

Come Worship the Baby

Cast: Three children, ages ten through twelve

Person 1—There was a baby born last night

Person 2—So what? Babies are born every day. Why are you announcing this one?

Person 3—Yeah! Give me a break. I see babies all the time.

Person 1—But this baby was born to be a king and a great ruler.

Person 2—You're talking crazy.

Person 3—We already have kings and great rulers. We don't need any more.

Person 1—But this one was born to rule throughout eternity. He will reign forever.

Person 2—Why are you all excited? We won't be around to see forever.

Person 3—Yeah! We'll be long gone by then.

Person 1—True. But we are around today, and we should go and worship the baby.

Person 2—Now you are *really* talking silly.

Person 3—I am not going to worship a baby!

Person 1—Well, let me tell you why and how this baby came into this world.

Person 2—(yawning) Boring!

Person 3—Do we have to hear this?

Person 1—No. But if you do, it will be a blessing to both of you.

Person 2—Can we at least sit down?

Person 3—Is this going to be a long story?

Person 1—Once you hear the story of baby Jesus, you'll understand.

(Person 2 and 3 sit.)

Person 1—There once was a woman whom God showed favor to bear his one and only son because God knew the world needed a Savior.

Person 2—I don't need a Savior.

Person 3—Me, either. I can save myself. I'm really strong. Look! See my muscles?

Person 1—Guys. Can I finish telling the story, please?

Person 2—Sure.

Person 3— Go ahead.

Person 1—The woman God found favor in was a virgin, but she would give birth to a baby. She was the chosen one.

Person 3—I bet she really felt special to be chosen by God.

Person 1—I'm sure she felt honored to give birth to this miracle baby.

Person 3—What makes this baby such a miracle?

Person 1—This baby came straight from God. He was conceived through the Holy Ghost. The power of God overshadowed her and she conceived. The baby would be born holy and would be called the son of God.

Person 2—What do you mean, he was born holy?

Person 1—He was born without sin because he was born through the Holy Ghost.

Person 3—Are we holy?

Person 1—No. We were born in sin.

Person 2—Why?

Person 1—Because we are descendants of Adam and Eve. They committed the first sin when they ate from the tree of knowledge. That is how sin entered the world. Adam and Eve were the first man and woman, and we were born through that linage. Therefore, we were born into sin. They had two boys, Cain and Abel. Cain committed the second sin when he killed his brother.

Person 2—Boy! This is getting interesting!

Person 3—So, because we were born in sin, the only one who can free us is the one who was born without sin.

Person 1—You're understanding it now. This is why baby Jesus is special: because he is the son of God and he was born without sin.

Person 3— So this baby was born for us because we were born in sin and today we are lost in sin.

Person 2—I don't understand how God could send his son to a world so cruel and mean.

Person 1—Only because he loves us and he want us to accept and love his only son.

Person 2—Can I be holy like Christ?

Person 3—Me too! After hearing all of this, I want to be like Jesus.

Person 1—You can accept Christ and try to become more like him each day. Because of sin we'll never be exactly like him. But once we accept Christ's death and resurrection, we will be saved through God's grace.

Person 2—What do you mean, Christ's death? Is Jesus going to die?

Person 1—Yes. He will die for us one day, but he will be resurrected. If we believe with all our hearts that we're sinners, and that Christ can save us because he is the son of God, then we are saved by God's grace.

Person 3—What is grace?

Person 1—Grace is the unmerited favor of God. We don't deserve it, but God loved us so he gave it to us.

Person 2—You mean we don't have to work to receive grace?

Person 1—That's right. It's a free gift from God.

Person 2—I really feel bad for what I said about this baby. God, please forgive me.

Person 3—Please forgive me too.

Person 1—He will if you mean it with all your heart.

Person 2—I do.

Person 3—I do too.

All—Now, can we all go and worship this baby? He has come to save us all.

POEMS AND SPEECHES

Watched from Above

Christ, our Savior, was born in the city of David.
From the time the king heard the news, Christ was hated.
An innocent baby loved by many and perfectly made,
God watched over him in his manger as he lay.
He knew he would protect him from harm's way.
That is why he led him to Bethlehem to stay.
For he loved his son and watched him night and day,
From his throne he sat and looked down with joy
And smiled at his wonderful and only baby boy.
For he knew the price his son would pay one day.
God knew that his son would be crucified on the cross.
He loved us and would save all who believed from being lost.

Jesus Is All You Need for Christmas

Christmas is a time when we enjoying giving.
It is also a time some just like receiving.
It's a time of year when kids are at their best.
They are asking parents for this and for that.
And parents are telling kids, "Just let me rest."
Mommies are asking daddies for diamonds and gold.
And daddies are saying, "My dear, whatever you want."
Throughout the years I've asked for many things.
But to all who hear my voice today,
Jesus is the way, the truth, and the life.
He is all you need for Christmas.

Christmas Thoughts

As I lay in my bed on Christmas night,
I thought about a baby born to bring light
Into a world that was filled with darkness.
I thought about a little boy who came to bring me happiness,
And how he gave me more than just happiness; he gave me joy.

I thought about how blessed Mary felt when she held her baby boy,
And how she must have given thanks to God above
For giving birth to this baby who had nothing but love
To share with a world full of sinners.
I thought about my heavenly Father and how he must have felt,
Sending his only begotten son to die to pay our debt.
I thought about how much God loved this world
And how he sent his precious son to die to prove it.
I thought about ways of showing him my love.
I'll just accept his only son he sent from above.

A Precious Gift

Who could have given a gift so wonderful?
A precious gift that would save the world,
A gift that is priceless and free,
One that God gave to you and me.

A precious gift we didn't have to buy,
But one that has bought us for a price.
A gift that was born to give his life,
That precious gift is Jesus Christ.

Please consider accepting this gift.
If you don't, you'll lose eternal life.
It's God's gift to us from above,
One that he truly gave out of love.

Mary, Mother of Jesus

Oh, how blessed was Mary,
To be chosen to carry the holy baby.
When the angel spoke to Mary,
She listened and obeyed.

God could have chose any woman
To carry and care for his only son.
But he wanted someone who was humble and meek,
Someone who was strong in faith and not weak.

Mary, oh, how you cared for him through his life,
Always loving him and doing what was right.
What an honor it must have been
To have given birth to the one who was free of sin.

Joseph, a Wise Man

An angel spoke to a man named Joseph one night in a dream.
He was a bit confused and wondered to himself, *What does this mean?*
Joseph, being a wise man, realized it was a message from God.
He listened, obeyed, and did what he was told.

At times he thought about what people in the town would say
Because Mary was with child and he had to marry her anyway.
Joseph, being a wise man, followed God's command
Because he truly understood and wanted to be part of God's plan.

Just like Mary, he knew she would give birth to our Savior.
Joseph realized why God had shown her great favor.
She was a woman with wisdom, meekness, and understanding,
Who was loved by God and Joseph, a wise man.

An Innocent Baby

We all were born innocent babies.
But there was something special about baby Jesus.
Maybe it's because he was born to live and then die for us,
And for that reason we can rejoice and be glad he was born.

An innocent baby who was born because of God's mercy,
He wanted to show the world just how much he cared.
What a blessing, an innocent baby for all to share.
Please accept him in your heart, and your life will be spared.

Do not harden your heart and forget this innocent baby,
One who came so you could have life more abundantly.
Oh, heavenly Father, what can we do to thank you?
"Not much," he says. "Just accept and love my only son."

For God promised if you love him with all your heart,
He will abide in you and will never depart.
Christ is the only answer for the world today.
Let him love and adore you in his special way.

Children, do you think that innocent baby grew up and disobeyed his parents?
No. Because we know that he was born without sin.
Can you all search your hearts from deep within?
Do you listen to your parents every now and then?

Or can you tell God that you have always obeyed?
We know that Christ obeyed his heavenly Father.
Christ is not happy with children who don't obey.
Please obey your parents, for Christ watches you each day.
God bless you.

Welcome His Birth

From the beginning God knew we would need a Savior.
He loved us and wanted to show us his favor.
God sent his only son to be born upon this earth.
Christ, we love you and we welcome your birth.

God loved us and didn't want death to be our fate.
He sent his son to be born in a world full of hate.
He knew Christ would suffer and die on the cross.
Why not accept him? He has already paid the cost.

He came that you and I may have a choice.
If he lives in your heart, be happy and rejoice
And know that eternal life is yours if you believe
That Christ was once dead, but today he lives.

Jesus Came to Give Us Hope

Before the birth of our Lord and Savior,
We were lost, and it showed in our behavior.
But today we know, if we believe,

We have hope and are not bound by chains and ropes.

Christ came to set us free and take our sins away.
If you will accept him and live for him each day,
You will be blessed with an abundance of love,
Sent down by our heavenly Father from above.

Christ is the hope that he came to give.
Though he died, yet he lives.
If we believe with all our heart,
He will give us hope and a new start.

Jesus Is Waiting

Jesus is waiting with open arms.
Come to him; he'll do you no harm.
He yearns to love and hold you tight.
Let him and you will see the light.
Jesus is waiting; please give him a chance.
Don't turn your back and walk away.
Just listen to what he has to say.
If you do, your life won't be such a mess.
Christ is waiting to love you more, not less.

Mary's Savior Too

One would have thought, when Mary gave birth to Christ, that
She would have done all she could to save his life.
But before Christ was conceived, Mary knew the reason for his birth.
She knew why God allowed his only son to be born upon this earth.

The angels told her, "Fear not! In you God has found favor."
Mary knew she would bring forth a son whose name would be Jesus.
A son of the Most High, who would be called our Savior.
Mary knew he would be King of all Kings and would reign forever.

In her spirit she rejoiced in God her Savior.
She knew she was blessed among all women.
God choose her to give birth to Christ, who would rule forever.

Mary accepted her blessing from God, who has everything in his hands.

God chose Mary to be Christ's mother, but Christ was Mary's Savior too.
She gave birth to the holy baby, but he is the only one who can save you.

A Love Song

Christ, when I am bored
And have nothing to do,
I can always sing
A love song to you.

King Jesus

To the King my heart I bring.
To this King a happy song I sing.
To this King I'll bow down and worship.
To this King I'll give thanks.
To this King I'll do a holy dance.
To this King I'll give a happy shout.
To this King, I know what you are about.
You are King Jesus without a doubt

A Talk with Christ

Christ, my Lord and Savior, you came right on time.
What a good feeling, knowing you came to be mine.
When I heard about your amazing birth, Christ,
It filled my heart with joy because I knew you came to pay the price
For sins I was lost in and didn't know which way to turn.

Now that you have come, in hell I won't have to burn.
Christ, if I can only get others to listen to me,
Then they will understand that you came to save the world.
Christ, I won't give up; I'll get them to see
That you were sent down from heaven to set them free.

God Spoke to Me

He said to me, "I sent my only son to you.
But you go around doing what you want to do.
Every day you choose to reject him.
That tells me you want to continue in sin.
I sent him to unloose you from ropes and chains.
But you say, 'No, I want to continue to do wrong.'
And I say to you, 'If you don't accept my son,
The payment for your rejection will be eternal death.'
I have spoken," says the Lord of Hosts.
"Make a choice, for the one you make will be yours."

If You Love Me, Share the Good News

You said that you loved Jesus Christ
And you were glad he came into your life.
You also said that you were glad he was born.
And that you would live your life for him and him alone.

Have you told Christ lately that you love him
And that you would do all you can to share the good news?
For Christ did not come to save only you.
Go out and share the news; start with one or two.

You have to be faithful to Christ and remain true.
Let others know they don't have to walk around feeling blue.
Christ was born on that cold Christmas night
So that they too could receive his precious light.

A Place Not Fit for a King

Joseph and Mary were in town one day,
Just to take care of some things, not to stay.
While they were there, the time had come
For Mary to give birth to the holy one.
They went to an inn for a room.
It was then they learned there were no more.

I can imagine they were in shock, with no place to go.
The innkeeper told them about an old stable next door.
Joseph took Mary in and laid her on the floor.
A few hours later, our Lord and Savior was born.
They had no place for him to lay his head.
Joseph found a manger and filled it with hay.
Mary wrapped him in swaddling clothes.
And there in the manger our Savior lay,
Born in a place not fit for a King.

Hallelujah

H is for hallelujah, Christ was born.
A is for the angles that watched over him.
L is for the love he came to give to us.
L is for the light we can see because he came.
E is for the everlasting life he was born to give.
L is for Lord, for he will be called Lord of Lords.
U is for the understanding he brings to the world.
J is for Jesus, who was born for you and me.
A is for the Almighty, born with all power in his hands.
H is for hallelujah, a Savior was born.

He Is Coming Back

Some believe Christ never died
On the cross,
So how could he
Come back to life?
Some say he is not a Savior,
That he is just a man
To whom God showed favor.
But I stand before you today
To tell you Christ did die on the cross,
And he was resurrected on the third day.
If you don't believe that he did,
Your soul is already lost.
Christ is coming back
For me and all who believe, and that is a fact.

My Prayer to Christ

Christ, I thank you for what you did
When you were nailed to the cross.
You did exactly what you said.
You took my sins along with you.
Christ, I thank you because
Dying is one thing you didn't have to do,
But you did it anyway
Because of the love you have for me
And you want to see me in heaven one day.
Thank you for this, Christ, I pray.

A Mother's Love

She must have felt such joy
To have given birth to a baby boy.
Mary knew it was a gift sent from above,
And she felt the goodness of a mother's love.

A mother's love is always caring,
Never selfish and always sharing.
Mary shared Jesus with the world
Because she knew one day he would save us all.

A mother's love means tears of joy.
Mary shed them when she held her baby boy.
She thanked God, who had shown her favor,
For Mary knew he was born to be our Savior.

Little Children, Come to Me

I can imagine Christ sitting down,
With little children gathered all around.
I know that Christ loves everyone,
But I believe children have a special place in his heart
Because they are innocent and have to be taught
The ways of Christ, our Lord and Savior.
I can hear Christ saying, "Little children, come to me.

What joy I get from seeing your faces.
Come to me and I will teach you my ways.
Little children, come to me when you hear my voice.
That will make me happy, and I will rejoice.
Please know that you are special to me.
If anyone hurts you, they won't go free.
Little children, come to me and know that I went to the cross.
I did it for you, and I've already paid the cost
For you and all who are lost in sin.
Do not be afraid, I will return again.

Jesus Is Alive and Waiting for You

Christ is alive and waiting for you with open arms.
He wants you to trust and believe in him; he'll do you no harm.
He yearns for you to do what is right and not give in to Satan's temptations
Because he wants to give you the gift of salvation.

With us he wants a personal relationship.
Just talk to him, pray to him, love him, and don't wait; just do it.
It is not Christ's desire for any of us to die and go to hell.
He commands us to abided in him and to do good as well.

I can imagine him sitting at the right hand of God the Father
With tears in his eyes because some of us don't want to be bothered.
Christ died to show us his unchanging love.
Will you accept him in your heart today and be blessed from above?

Mary's Broken Heart

Mary stood near the cross with tears in her eyes.
She watched in disbelief as Christ died.
She knew that for the world this was a new start.
But that thought couldn't heal Mary's broken heart.
I can imagine she cried out, "Please help my son."
In her heart she knew the reason he'd been born.
She realized this was the day he had to depart.
But nothing could be said to heal Mary's broken heart.

Things Christ May Have Said to His Father

Father, I love you and only you I want to please.
I prayed to you, Father, and this is the answer I received.
Yes, Father, I will go to the cross and my life I will give
Because I know this is your holy and divine will.
I will listen and obey because I know this is right.
And when I return, the world will see me as their light.
For if I don't obey you, my precious Father,
Then how can I expect the world to choose me to follow?

Jesus Is with Me

When I get up in the morning,
Jesus is there, and he asks how I am doing.
When I get on the bus to go to school,
He sits next to me and tells me I am cool.
When I get to my classroom
And my teacher is having a bad day,
Jesus, maybe you can tell her that you are the way.
When I get home and start my homework,
Jesus hugs me and tells me I am smart.
And when I kneel to say my prayers at night,
He tells me he loves me and to sleep tight.

Christ, Can You Walk with Me?

My burdens are heavy and unbearable sometimes.
People laugh and tell me I am out of my mind
Because I believe that Christ died on the cross for me.
They say I am silly for believing that, and how could that be?
Sometimes I feel like I am all alone.
Why can't people believe what Christ has done?
Christ, my heart is heavy; can you walk with me?
"Sure," he says, "because I am the one who died to set you free."

Christ's Walk to the Cross

The crowd grew larger and the line got longer.

One can only imagine how lonely Christ must have felt.
His walk to the cross was painful and he had no help.
He was made to carry his cross on his back.
Christ never complained, and no questions did he ask.
I know his walk to the cross wasn't an easy one.
Some in the crowd were angry, some glad, and some mourned
Because he was beaten so badly and scorned.
But Christ remained obedient, never forgetting why he was born.

Christ's Thoughts on the Cross

As I looked around at the people in the crowd,
I saw some who were sad and some who were proud.
Oh, no, and there is my mother with tears in her eyes.
Mother, please don't cry, because you know why
My heavenly Father said that I must die:
To save a world he cares so much for.
Therefore, I must die and you must understand why.

He Came Back to life

Jesus was once dead.
I saw him hang his head.
Three days later he came back to life.
He was among his people for a while.
Then he ascended back into heaven
To prepare a place for all who believe
That he was once dead but came back to life.

If I Could Have Carried His Cross

Christ was beaten brutally all night long.
The next morning he was kicked and beaten again.
How can they do all these things to an innocent man?
Next they put on his head a crown made of thorns.
Then he was given his cross to carry alone.
Christ, if could, I would have carried your cross.
Then they led him down a road and up Calvary's hill.

Seeing all of this made it hard for me to stand still.
Christ, I am sad and hurt for what you went through.
If I could have carried your cross, I would have.

Father, I Will Do Your Will

Christ faithfully prayed in the garden that night.
He wanted to be sure what God was saying was right.
Christ asked his Father many times for his will.
"Father, please show me your purpose for my life."
After many hours of praying to his Father,
He received the answer in the garden, and he stood still.
He looked toward heaven and said, "Father, I will do your will."

To the Thief on the Cross

"I see you have broken one of God's ten commandments."
Yes, my Lord, I did, but in my heart I have repented.
My Lord, why are you on a cross next to me, a thief?
"It is my Father's will that I die on the cross.
When I do, the world will be saved and not lost.
Through my death on the cross, I will take on all sins."
My Lord, I know I have sinned, but I have opened my heart and let you in.
"Then truly we will be together today in paradise."

Peace, Love, and Joy

Christ has peace; I have peace.
Christ has love; I have love.
Christ has joy; I have joy.
Thank you, Jesus Christ.
You have made me a happy boy.

I Watched and I Listened

Christ, I listened to you pray.
Christ, I listened to you teach.
Christ, I listened to your stories.

Christ, I watched as you carried
Your cross up a hill so very high.
Christ, I watched you as you died.
And I watched as you ascended into the sky.

The End Has Come

To my faithful disciples,
The time has come
For me to leave you.
You must remain true
To yourselves and all you teach.
I want you to go out and preach
My word to all who will listen:
"Do not let your hearts be heavy.
Remember the good times we shared,
And always know that I cared.
I go to prepare a place.
I know you will miss seeing my face.
I will not leave you alone.
But my work down here is done.
My Holy Spirit will descend
And will guide you until the end.
Bless you, my good and faithful men."

I Will Return

Even though I may ascend and go away,
I will return for you one day
Do not be sad and heavy burdened,
And do not let your heart be hardened.
For I go away to prepare a place.
Oh, what joy you will have when you see my face,
When I return to gather my faithful sheep.

Stop Beating Him

I stood in the back of the crowd.
I saw them beat him until he fell to the ground.
He got up and was beaten to his knees.

I heard a voice cry out, "Stop beating him, please."
I moved from the back to a different place
Because I wanted to see my Savior's face.
His body was bloody, battered, and bruised.
I cried to them, "Stop beating him, please."
By then my Lord and Savior was tired and weak.
But He continued to walk up Calvary's hill
Because he knew this was his Father's will.

Christ Is Always with Me

When I wake up in the morning, he is by my side.
Christ is with me at school, and his love I cannot hide.
When I sit down to bless and eat my lunch,
I know that he is with me and I have to thank him a bunch.

When others talk about me and do bad things to me, I am not afraid,
Because Christ is with me and he will protect me, he said.
When I go to bed I pray to him at night,
For I know he will lead and guide me to do what is right.

I Wish

When I say I have a Savior,
I wish people would believe me.
When I say Christ died on the cross,
I wish they wouldn't laugh
And say that it is false.
I wish, when Christ comes back for me,
That they would see I was telling the truth.
I wish that it isn't too late.
But I know, for some, it will be.
And they won't enter into the gate.

Can I See Your Hands?

I heard about a man
Who was nailed to a cross,

A man who died in agony and pain.
I didn't believe, as I was thinking,
What did he have to gain?
As I was walking down a road,
I heard one person say to another,
"There is the man who died and arose.
There was something different about this man.
So I went to him and asked, 'Can I see your hands?'
He showed his hands to me.
There were holes, I could plainly see.
At the moment all I could say was,
'I believe. I believe. I believe.' "

He Is All You Need

Christ is my life.
Christ is my friend.
Christ my Savior.
Christ is able
To do all things.
If you put your trust in him,
He is all you need.

Pride

Before Christ died
I was lost in my pride.
I didn't need a Savior.
Why go to the cross for me?
I have money; that's all I need.
I don't need anything for free.

But now I realize how wrong I was
For thinking in such a foolish way.
Christ died to save me from my sins,
Something I surely cannot do on my own.

Now that I know I cannot save myself,
That pride I had is long gone.

Pray in Jesus' Name

Christ, when I'm sad,
And things are not going right,
It gives me comfort
To know, when I say
My prayers at night,
I can pray in your name and
You will make everything right.

He Listens

When I talk to Christ,
He always listens to me
Because he knows my heart,
and he knows that he is first
in my life.
Thank you, Christ,
for always listening
to what I have to say.

When You Bless Me

Christ, when you bless me,
I won't keep it to myself.
I will go out and tell everyone.
I will include the rich and the poor,
Because the poor may know you
And trust you, but they have a need for more.
And the rich may not know you,
And they just don't know
That you, Christ, would be
A blessing to them.
If they forget about their riches
And worship you and open their
Hearts and let you in,
Then they too can receive a blessing from heaven.

I Will Follow You Forever

Christ, I've never been one to follow.
I've always wanted to be a leader.
Now I realize, since I have accepted you,
That you have the right to tell me what to do.
Now I have peace in being a follower.
As long as I know that you will be my leader,
I will follow you forever.

There Is Joy in Knowing Christ

Throughout my life I've have some happiness.
I've had some good days, and some were bad.
Whatever I did, I gave it my best.
I realize now some of my choices weren't good.
But today I can be happy and rejoice,
Because one day I heard a voice,
One that said, "Come to me, my precious child.
If you follow me, you will have joy."
Today I know there is joy in knowing Christ.

Christ Is

Christ is our Lord and only Savior.
Christ is the one who asked God to show us favor.
Christ is righteousness and goodness; he came to teach.
Christ is our innocent Savior, whose love we seek.
Christ is our Lord, the one who is strong and not weak.
Christ is a teacher who taught us to love one another.
Christ is merciful and shows it in a special way.
Christ is the one who abides in us each day.
Christ is the Shepherd whose sheep know his voice.
Christ is always with us, and for that we can rejoice.
Christ is our only intercessor; his promises he keeps.
Christ is the one who never leaves his sheep.
Christ is the only hope for the world today.

IT TOUCHED MY HEART (A True Story)

Once, when I was teaching Children's Church, I met a little girl who had never attended church. Oh, how it touched me as I wondered how that could be. She told me she had never heard of Christ. Tears covered my eyes as I stood there, wondering why. I knew at that moment she needed to hear about our Savior.

As I told her about how Christ died on the cross for our sins, her eyes lit up. She was amazed at what was being said. She wanted to hear more. I was excited as I told the story. The little girl was pleased that I, along with the other kids in children's church, would take the time to tell her how and why Christ came to earth. I told her about his amazing birth. Then I asked her if she knew about sin. She had a confused look on her little face. I thought, *Boy, is she in the right place!*

I had all the kids explain to her the meaning of sin. Afterward, she had a clear understanding. She also understood that if she believed in Christ, he would remove all her sin.

I asked her if she was familiar with heaven and hell. I saw another puzzled look on her face, and all the kids raised their hands to be the first to tell her about the wonderful kingdom of God as well as how awful Satan's home in hell will be for unbelievers.

By the time service ended, she knew exactly who Christ was and why he came to earth. The children and I felt blessed because we had done what Christ commanded us to do. You see, Christ wants us to go out and share the good news.

God is smiling on my class of little warriors for Jesus. That Sunday morning proved to be a blessing not only for the little girl who visited our class, but for the students as well. They got a chance to see that there are people in the world who haven't heard about God's goodness, grace, and mercy. They learned how important it is to share the Word of God with those who may not know him.

May God continue to bless the little girl who visited our class that Sunday and continue to bless my class as they grow in the knowledge of our Lord Jesus Christ.

FATHER, PLEASE BLESS THIS BOOK

Our heavenly Father, who art in heaven, I thank you for inspiring and giving me the wisdom, knowledge, and understanding to write this book. Father, I prayed and asked you to reveal your will and purpose for my life. You listened and answered, and I obeyed. This book is your will, and I ask you to please bless it.

Father, I thank you for revealing part of your will to me. I will continue to pray and ask for more of your will, because I know that you have a lot of work for me to do to further your kingdom. Now, Father, I pray this book will reach many people and touch many hearts. I also pray that through this book many lives will be saved. I pray that many will ask, "What must I do to be saved?" Father, you know my heart, and that is my purpose for writing this book.

Father, once again, I thank you for inspiring me to write this book to share the good news about our Lord and Savior. Please bless this book in Jesus' name. Amen.

QUESTIONS & COMMENTS

The author, Pearl Robinson can be reached by email for any questions or comments concerning my book! I am looking forward to hearing from some of you! God Bless you all! The email is pearl043@aol.com

Printed in the United States
28160LVS00006B/499-537

9 780976 375678